The ART *of*
TOPIARY

The ART of
TOPIARY

poems by

JAN WAGNER

translated from the german by

DAVID KEPLINGER

MILKWEED EDITIONS

Achtzehn Pasteten / *Australien*: © Hanser Berlin im Carl Hanser Verlag München, 2015
First published in German by Berlin Verlag, 2007 / 2010
Regentonnenvariationen: © Hanser Berlin im Carl Hanser Verlag München, 2014
© 2017, English translation by David Keplinger

Published 2017 by Milkweed Editions
Printed in the United States of America
Cover design by Mary Austin Speaker
Cover cyanotype by Anna Atkins
Author photo by Alberto Novelli
Translator photo by Czarina Divinagracia
17 18 19 20 21   5 4 3 2 1
First Edition

Milkweed Editions, an independent nonprofit publisher, gratefully acknowledges sustaining support
from the Jerome Foundation; the Lindquist & Vennum Foundation; the McKnight Foundation;
the National Endowment for the Arts; the Target Foundation; and other generous contributions
from foundations, corporations, and individuals. Also, this activity is made possible by the voters of
Minnesota through a Minnesota State Arts Board Operating Support grant, thanks to a legislative
appropriation from the arts and cultural heritage fund, and a grant from Wells Fargo. For a full
listing of Milkweed Editions supporters, please visit milkweed.org.

Library of Congress Cataloging-in-Publication Data

Names: Wagner, Jan, 1971- author. | Keplinger, David, 1968 - translator.
Title: The art of topiary : poems / Jan Wagner ; translated by David
    Keplinger.
Description: Minneapolis, Minnesota : Milkweed editions, 2017. | Includes
    bibliographical references. | Parallel texts in German and English.
Identifiers: LCCN 2017007196 (print) | LCCN 2017010113 (ebook) | ISBN
    9781571314963 (pbk. : alk. paper) | ISBN 9781571319715 (ebook)
Classification: LCC PT2685.A4444 A2 2017 (print) | LCC PT2685.A4444 (ebook) |
    DDC 833/.92--dc23
LC record available at https://lccn.loc.gov/2017007196

Milkweed Editions is committed to ecological stewardship. We strive to align our book
production practices with this principle, and to reduce the impact of our operations in
the environment. We are a member of the Green Press Initiative, a nonprofit coalition of
publishers, manufacturers, and authors working to protect the world's endangered forests and
conserve natural resources. *The Art of Topiary* was printed on acid-free 100% postconsumer-
waste paper by Thomson-Shore.

contents

II

III

The ART *of*
TOPIARY

Translating [with] Jan Wagner

Tonight I walked out to see the moon, five days after winter solstice, hung in the blue hour of twilight, a sliver of luminosity along the rim of its circumference from about the three o'clock position to eight o'clock. It was just enough for me to catch the sense of the whole orb: part illusion, part literal translation of light on the rods and cones of the retina.

I got to thinking about how the suggestion of a presence is sometimes more striking than the thing itself—a theme that surfaces in my personal tastes, from Picasso to Miles Davis—as I turned to complete the last drafts of these translations with German poet Jan Wagner. Wagner is not readily categorized. He employs forms as he needs them and escapes their requirements when necessary. In our exchanges he has described his attitude toward traditional forms as a kind of corset the poem is trying to undo.

As Wagner's collaborator in English—I prefer this term; I speak no German—it was not a shared language but our affection for the rising and falling of iambic rhythm, the music of traditional rhymed forms, and haunting Modernist imagery that united us toward our goal. Here are sonnets such as "rhino," in which a flitting buphagus lives atop the armored plane of the rhino's back; rhymed quatrains in which Lazarus's legendary resurrection is set against a backdrop of grocery store queues and alleyways; the sestina, this book's title poem, in which the repeated words from the German describe a garden that eats its creator; a long haiku series on rain barrels; strict sapphic odes that sing of a "free-for-all in the bar poseidon"; and free verse, as in the "essay" series.

Free verse remains as difficult to translate in Wagner as the formal poems. For example, "essay on gnats" must produce the formal aura of antiquity—with its references to sphinxes and the

Rosetta stone—without using repetition, meter, or rhyme. The poem concludes on an image of hovering gnats as a "rosetta stone, without the stone." What they translate is the ephemeral.

Like the moon in tonight's post-solstice sky, the translator is given to create through a sliver of literalness the illusion of the entire circumference—that is, the work's denotation, connotation, and form. Thus in the piece called "gecko," a prose poem, my work involved reproducing the alliteration, assonance, and consonance of Wagner's original, a heightened sense of language that harkens back to the four-beat Anglo-Saxon line of *Beowulf.* I have attempted to stay as faithful to Wagner's rhyme schemes as possible (with some variation by necessity). Further, I have tried to honor his technique of splitting words between line breaks. The reader will note that our English split words are not the same, in most cases, as his German; but in the spirit of his voice and his prosody, I have attempted to create a similar effect.

Now and then I have released a poem from the corset altogether, as in the final line of "amish," which abandons its rhyme scheme so as not to sacrifice sense on some fundamental level. And sometimes, with Wagner collaborating, I have changed the sense to allow important formal qualities to live on the page in the way the author intended. This happened mostly in rhymed sequences, as in the last line of "rhino":

with this one bird, the buphagus,

which balances onto the square of his back
like a single piece of sevres china,
a demitasse cup, fragile, precarious.

"Precarious" does not appear in the German; but the efg/efg rhyme scheme remained vital to the piece—a lumbering rhino all the while as graceful as a dancer balancing a demitasse cup—and because Wagner and I agreed that the word "buphagus" should be saved for the last moment of the penultimate stanza, a Latinate "-ious" word was added as the closing note.

With the author as my collaborator, I have strived to maintain a balance between the demands of our two languages. More than in my previous books of translations, I found it necessary to rewrite, with the author, an English version neither mine nor his, but ours.

For those fluent in but not native to the German language, it will be helpful to read the source material for sound and sense, then return to our versions, where we seek to recreate for English readers the logic of Wagner's imagery, the antique voice that invades upon the modern, and subtle departures from form. Yet what you will find in the English is, as stated, a slightly altered Wagner. We have sometimes leaned toward an allegiance to music and form and, when necessary, drifted from a literal representation of the original. Over the years, our many connotative, literal, and formal versions of each poem allowed me ever closer glimpses of their source. Reading Rilke as a young poet I knew that the real Rilke was nowhere to be found but in the German; I read all the available Rilkes; I read the originals to feel them in my mouth. I read with the understanding that in the center of this array of Rilkes lay the one Rilke whose music sometimes found my ear at the unconscious level.

That was the idea here. We have tried to create a system of checks and balances that apportion power equally among connotation, form, and literalness. Often Wagner and I would exchange half a dozen versions of a piece before settling on one crystallized draft. We worked entirely by correspondence. We began our collaboration in early 2009. We completed the last of these translations in late 2016.

Jan Wagner was born in 1971 and lives in Berlin, enjoying a reputation as one of Germany's most celebrated younger poets.

He has won the Ernst Meister Award for Poetry (2005) and the Wilhelm Lehmann Award (2009), and he has published six collections, most recently *Rain Barrel Variations* (2014).

David Keplinger
Washington, DC, 2017

I

nashorn

komm näher. seine augen sind zu stumpf,
um etwas zu erkennen außer schatten, dem geflimmer
von gras und hitze — und dem horn: ihm stampft
es hinterher wie schlafende dem finger

des hypnotiseurs. nicht eine wolke gleitet
über die ebene, während es trinkt,
zum nächsten schlammloch weiterzieht — gekleidet
in gleichmut, eine haut, die nichts durchdringt — ,

sein tonnengrau durch die vergeß-
lichkeit von jahrmillionen schleppt, allein
mit jenem vogel: der buphagus,

den es auf seinem rücken balanciert
wie ein stück sèvres-porzellan,
    ein mokkatässchen, überraschend zart.

rhino

come closer. his eyes are too dull,
depicting nothing besides shadows, the glitter
of grass and heat—and the horn: he tramples
after it like sleepers follow the finger

of the hypnotist. not a cloud is gliding
over the plain, while he drinks,
travels to the next mud hole—hiding
himself in indifference, impermeable skin—

his heft of pure gray lugs through black
ages, the millions of forgetful years, alone
with this one bird, the buphagus,

which balances onto the square of his back
like a single piece of sevres china,
        a demitasse cup, fragile, precarious.

gecko

sitzt plötzlich dort, als das licht angeht, eilt über die wand:
ein wandernder riß, der sich hinten schließt, während er
in laufrichtung das weiß zerteilt, rot und pulsierend, eine
winzige lavaspalte. was man im schatten des ätna erzählt:
daß er nur die wohnungen solcher menschen aufsucht, die
freundlichen geistes sind. die dächer von syrakus, die wellen
vor messina. tage später sein heller bauch auf dem kiesweg —
und binnen stunden ein brodeln von ameisen, das seine form
perfekt imitiert, eine wimmelnde mimikry. kieloben liegt das
sizilianische fischerboot am strand, ein wrack, seine rippen
porös und ausgebleicht von der sonne. am morgen darauf
nichts als das zierliche rückgrat, ein verschwindend weißes
stäbchen, das übrigbleibt; ein bloßer zahnstocher im breiten
maul des august.

gecko

suddenly stands there when the light snaps on, hurrying over the wall: a wandering crack that heals itself from behind, while opening the plaster in front of him, running. a throbbing, reddish, tiny gash of lava. a story told in the shadow of etna: how he visits only the houses of people with a gracious, gentle spirit. the rooftops of syracuse; the waves of messina. days later: his translucent belly on the gravel path—and within an hour, a seething of ants, exactly imitating his form, their teeming mimicry. overturned lies this sicilian skiff on its beach, wrecked, its ribs porous and bleached by sun. the morning after, nothing but the nuance of a spine, a vanishing white wand that remains. a mere toothpick in the broad maw of august.

quittenpastete
Aus dem Zyklus: "Achtzehn Pasteten"

wenn sie der oktober ins astwerk hängte,
ausgebeulte lampions, war es zeit: wir
pflückten quitten, wuchteten körbeweise
⠀⠀gelb in die küche

unters wasser. apfel und birne reiften
ihrem namen zu, einer schlichten süße —
anders als die quitte an ihrem baum im
⠀⠀hintersten winkel

meines alphabets, im latein des gartens,
hart und fremd in ihrem arom. wir schnitten,
viertelten, entkernten das fleisch (vier große
⠀⠀hände, zwei kleine),

schemenhaft im dampf des entsafters, gaben
zucker, hitze, mühe zu etwas, das sich
roh dem mund versagte. wer konnte, wollte
⠀⠀quitten begreifen,

ihr gelee, in bauchigen gläsern für die
dunklen tage in den regalen aufge-
reiht, in einem keller von tagen, wo sie
⠀⠀leuchteten, leuchten.

quince paté
From the series "Eighteen Pies"

when october hung them in the branches,
bulging lanterns, it was time: quinces,
we plucked quinces, heaving in our baskets
    yellows to the kitchen

and into water. pear and apple ripened
toward their names, to a simple sweetness—
different from the quinces on their branches
    hanging in far corners

of my alphabet, in the garden's latin,
hard and foreign in aroma: we sliced,
quartered, cored the flesh (four huge
    hands, two smaller ones)

shadowed in the juicer steam, added
sugar, heat, effort toward something
so raw it resisted the mouth. who could or would want
    to understand quinces,

jellies set in bulbous jars for the
darkest days, lined up on our shelves in
a basement of such days, where they
    shone, are still shining.

versuch über mücken

als hätten sich alle buchstaben
auf einmal aus der zeitung gelöst
und stünden als schwarm in der luft;

stehen als schwarm in der luft,
bringen von all den schlechten nachrichten
keine, dürftige musen, dürre

pegasusse, summen sich selbst nur ins ohr;
geschaffen aus dem letzten faden
von rauch, wenn die kerze erlischt,

so leicht, daß sich kaum sagen läßt: sie sind,
erscheinen sie fast als schatten,
die man aus einer anderen welt

in die unsere wirft; sie tanzen,
dünner als mit bleistift gezeichnet
die glieder; winzige sphinxenleiber;

der stein von rosetta, ohne den stein.

essay on gnats

as if every character had fled
all at once from the newspaper
and hovered as a swarm in the air,

they hover as a swarm in the air,
transmitting from the awful news
nothing. prudent muses, emaciated

pegasusses humming nothing but themselves
into the ear; borne of the last band
of smoke when the candle is snuffed,

and so weightless it's hardly possible to say:
they are. appearing more as shadow
from an alternate world

now cast into ours, they dance,
limbs now so thin as if drawn
with a pencil; tiny sphinxes are their bodies;

rosetta stone, without the stone.

holunder

für Richard Pietraß

wofür die tinte, fragt man, im geäst
die schwarzen tropfen, die sich unverhofft
zum amselklecks verdichten? welcher text
für welches grundbuch, welches heft?

neben der alten scheune, wo in den beeten
das land versickert, hinterm zaun. der duft
der doldenrispen im april, das bütten-
papier, das er aus seinen tiefen schöpft,

während die wäsche trocknet, an der stange
zu flattern beginnt, die amseln sich in dohlen
verwandeln. welches süße oder strenge
geheimnis, fragt man, wird er mit uns teilen,

wenn wir im herbst ums dunkel der terrinen
versammelt sind, mit unseren blankgeputzten
silberlöffeln, jenen allzureinen
sonntagshemden, schweigsam wie kopisten?

elderflower

for Richard Pietraß

why this ink, you ask, in the branches,
black droplets that spontaneously assume
a blackbird's splotch? which entries
for which land register? which volume?

near the aging barn, where the land is draining
into flower beds, behind the fence. the scent
of clustered flower stalks in april, the linen
paper that he scoops from his own depth,

while the laundry is drying out on the line,
starting to flutter a little, the blackbirds turning .
into choughs. what secret, sweet or severe,
will he share with us, you might inquire,

when you gather around the dark of tureens
in autumn, with meticulously polished
silver spoons, those all-too-clean
sunday shirts as silent as copyists?

dezember 1914

"One of the nuts belonging to the regiment got out of the trenches and started to walk toward the German lines."

natürlich dachten wir, daß sie plemplem
geworden waren, als sie ungeschützt
aus ihrer deckung traten, nur mit plum-
pudding und mistelzweig — doch kein geschütz

schlug an. wir trafen sie im niemandsland,
unschlüssig was zu tun sei, zwischen gräben
und grenzen, schlamm und draht, und jede hand
an ihrer hosennaht. bis wir die gaben

verteilten: einer hatte zigaretten
dabei und einer bitterschokolade,
ein dritter wußte mittel gegen ratten
und läuse. die an diesem punkt noch lade-

hemmung hatten, zückten nach dem rum
familienfotos, spielten halma
und standen lärmend, wechselten reihum
adressen, uniformen, helme,

bis kaum etwas im schein der leuchtspurgarben
auf diesem aufgeweichten, nackten anger
zu tauschen übrig blieb außer den gräben
im rücken, ihrem namenlosen hunger.

december 1914

"One of the nuts belonging to the regiment got out of the trenches and started to walk toward the German lines."

plemplem, we imagined them, of course,
as each and every one, without protection,
stepped from the regiment, holding christmas
pudding, sprigs of mistletoe—yet, no gun

blasted. we met them out in no-man's-land,
unsure of what to do, between the trenches
and the borders, mud and wire, and every hand
against its holster as the other unclenched

the alms: one gave us of his cigarettes.
a second knew the remedies for rats
and lice. another had dark chocolate.
whoever in the group that couldn't yet

unjam his inhibition now took out rum
and family pictures, played a round of halma
as we gathered noisily exchanging names
and home addresses, uniforms and helmets,

so barely one more thing within the banks
of light, along this rain-wet, naked pasture,
was left to be exchanged—except the trenches
dug in back of us, their nameless hunger.

der westen

der fluß denkt in fischen. was war es also,
das sergeant henley ihm als erster
entriß, die augen gelb und starr, die barteln
zwei schürhaken ums aschengraue maul,
das selbst die hunde winseln ließ?

die stromschnellen und ihre tobende
grammatik, der wir richtung quelle folgen.
die dunstgebirge in der ferne,
die ebenen aus gras und ab und zu
ein eingeborener, der amüsiert
zu uns herüberschaut und dann
im wald verschwindet: all das tragen wir
in adams alte karte ein, benennen
arten und taten. fieber in den muskeln
und über wochen die diät aus wurzeln
und gottvertrauen. unterm hemd die zecken
wie abstecknadeln auf der haut: so nimmt
die wildnis maß an uns.

seltsames gefühl: die grenze
zu sein, der punkt, an dem es endet und
beginnt. am feuer nachts kreist unser blut
in wolken von moskitos über uns,
während wir mit harten gräten
die felle aneinandernähen, schuhe
für unser ziel und decken für die träume.
voraus das unberührte, hinter uns
die schwärmenden siedler, ihre charta

the west

the river thinks in fish. what was it then
that sergeant henley snatched from it,
the eyes yellow and torpid, the barbs
of two pokers around the ash-gray jaw,
which even caused the dogs to whine?

white rapids and their raging grammar
which we trace to the river's source.
the smoky mountains out beyond us,
the plains of grass and now and then
a native who with amusement
takes a look at us and disappears
into the forest. all that we chart
on adam's old map, we classify
as breed or deed. the feverish sweat.
our diet of root and faith. beneath
our shirts the ticks affixed like pins
into the skin: so the wilderness
carefully takes our measurements.

the oddest feeling: to be the edge,
the point at which the frontier ends and
begins. around the fire at night our blood
circles in clouds of mosquitoes above us,
while with sturdy fish bones we sew furs
to one another, shoes for our journey
and heavy blankets for the dreams.
ahead of us the untouched. behind us
the swarming settlers and their charters

aus zäunen und gattern; hinter uns
die planwagen der händler,
die großen städte, voller lärm und zukunft.

drawn up by fences and gates. behind us
the merchants' covered wagons, the
enormous cities, full of noise and future.

wejherowo

"No one left and no one came"
—EDWARD THOMAS

ich erinnere mich an wejherowo,
den namen jedenfalls — und das gebräunte
schild überm steig. kein windhauch, keine rufe,
nur dieser julihimmel, sein sechssiebtel-
gewitterdunkel. eine hummel brannte
wie eine zündschnur langsam durchs abteil.

ein stand mit kirschen, seine kühle wage
aus silber, in der ferne ein paar kräne
auf viertel vor sechs. das räuspern im waggon,
die feinen risse draußen im asphalt —
das gras darunter setzte seine grüne
brechstange an. und immer noch das schild,

nirgendwo anders als in wejherowo:
ein schwarzer himmel, alle fahnen schlaff,
die kirschen immer praller, immer reifer,
als unser schaffner, rot wie ein gepei-
nigter, den steig betrat. ein schriller pfiff,
und die landschaft eilte von allen seiten herbei.

wejherowo

"No one left and no one came."
—EDWARD THOMAS

i have a memory: wejherowo,
the name, at any rate, and the bronze
signpost at the tracks. no wind, no voice,
only this july-sky, this eighty-five-percent-
chance-of-storm-sky. a bumblebee's fuse
burning down, slow, in the compartment.

a stand with bags of cherries, its cold scale
made of silver. in the distance a few cranes
at quarter to six. the rasping of a throat
in the neighboring cabin; the fine cracks in asphalt
outside—the grass within just starting to wrench
its green crowbar. and still the signpost

nowhere else than in wejherowo:
a black sky, all the flags impotent,
the cherries more firm, more ripe than ever,
as our conductor, red like someone in torment,
stepped out onto the track. a whistle sounded.
from every side of us, the landscape hastened.

teebeutel

I

nur in sackleinen
gehüllt. kleiner eremit
in seiner höhle.

II

nichts als ein faden
führt nach oben. wir geben
ihm fünf minuten.

teabag

I

a swathe of linen
all there is to cover him,
hermit in his cave.

II

nothing other than
a string leads out. we give him
four to five minutes.

augustín lópez: the art of topiary
Aus dem Zyklus: "drei mögliche bücher"

er machte sich im morgengrauen ans werk,
wenn alles schlief. bei sonne oder regen
war er dort draußen, ließ den wilden buchs
durch ringe springen, schnitt ihn längs der gatter
als kugel, pyramide, säulengarten
zurecht: so hörten wir die ganze zeit

die schere, sahen, wie er ohne sinn und zeit
für anderes natur mit drähten oder werg
in neue formen zwang: ein irrgarten
mit minotaurus und der goldregen
der danae; ein tor mit fallgatter,
dann türme, mauern, bis sich in dem buchs

das panorama einer ganzen stadt aus buchs
eröffnete, vor der zur sommerzeit
auf einem grünen meer eine regatta
von buchsfregatten kreuzte. jeden werk-
tag, sogar sonntags ging er in regen-
tenhaltung durch sein weites reich, den garten,

doch eines morgens war es still im garten.
ein leichter wind nur nestelte am buchs,
trimmte die blätter. wozu aufregen?
verschwanden nicht die künstler jeder zeit
am ende hinter ihrem eigenen werk?
wir standen lange vor dem eisengatter,

dann trauten sich zwei jungen übers gatter
zu steigen, fanden schließlich dort im garten

augustín lópez: the art of topiary
From the series "three possible books"

he set out every dawn to do his work
while everyone was sleeping. in sun and rain
the man was there, to make the wild box
jump through rings, cutting it along the gates
into globes, into pyramids, column gardens,
just so: so we heard him keeping time

with scissors, saw how, sacrificing time
for anything else, he willed with wirework
the natural world into new forms: gardens
of labyrinths, minotaurs, and the golden rain
of danae; with portcullis gates,
then towers, walls, so that, as if by bricks,

the landscape of a fabulous city, boxed
by walls, emerged. it was met at that time
by a topiary sea, upon which crossed frigates
of tree-envoys. the days he did his work,
even sunday, he went as one who reigns
over a vast kingdom, postured in his garden

as its king until just silence was its guardian.
only a light wind twitched the wild box,
trimmed at its leaves. why should we rant
about this? don't all artists at some time
or other dissolve into their work?
we stood for a while in front of the gates,

then two boys dared to climb over. agape
they found surrounded by gardens

ein männerbildnis als sein letztes werk,
und tief darin als herz, versteckt im buchs,
ein vogelnest zu kalter jahreszeit.
die eier wie aus marmor, wie von regen

gesprenkelt, hart — und nichts schien sich zu regen,
wenn man an ihnen lauschte. die ergatter-
ten stücke hingen in der weihnachtszeit
am christbaum, doch von ihm und seinem garten
kein wort mehr. bald schon sahen wir am buchs
die jungen triebe wachsen, war das buschwerk

von regen üppig. so verging sein werk,
und mit der zeit vergaßen wir den garten.
hinter dem gatter draußen blüht der buchs.

a gentleman's image as his last great work,
and within it as the heart, hidden in the box,
a bird's nest left from wintertime.
the eggs the color of marble, rain-

flecked, hard—and nothing seemed to rouse
when one listened to them. we gathered
fallen pieces for the tree at christmastime.
but from the master gardener and his garden,
no more words. soon we saw that on the box
young shoots were growing, the work

of nourishing rain. so the garden's details faded
and in time we would forget his work.
behind the gates burst flowers from the box.

chamäleon

älter als der bischofsstab,
den es hinter sich herzieht, die krümme
des schwanzes. komm herunter, rufen wir
ihm zu auf seinem ast, während die zunge
als teleskop herausschnellt, es das sternbild
einer libelle frißt: ein astronom
mit einem blick am himmel und dem andern
am boden — so wahrt es den abstand
zu beiden. die augenkuppeln, mit schuppen
gepanzert, eine festung, hinter der
nur die pupille sich bewegt, ein nervöses
flackern hinter der schießscharte (manchmal
findet man seine haut wie einen leeren
stützpunkt, eine längst geräumte these).
komm herunter, rufen wir. doch es regt
sich nicht, verschwindet langsam zwischen
den farben. es versteckt sich in der welt.

chameleon

older than the bishop's staff
which it drags, right to the crook,
behind itself. come down to us, we call
upward to its perch when the tongue,
become a telescope, shoots out, devours
a constellation's butterfly, astronomer
with one gaze toward the sky and the other
to the ground—thus keeping its distance
from both. the eye's cupola, armored
with scales, a fortress; behind which
only the pupil moves, a nervous
glittering within its loopholes (some days
you come across its skin like an empty
barracks, a long-abandoned belief). come down,
we call. but it doesn't move, slowly disappears
between the colors, hiding in the world.

tarock

seit jahren kein schuß. nur diese großen pilze,
die schatten der tellerminen, die der erde
im grenzstreifen entwachsen, und der plötzli-
che krach am frühen morgen, eine herde
versprengter schafe. aus den kalenderblättern
ragen die alpen. die drei soldaten spielen.

tage, nächte — mit den sternbildern
des stacheldrahts darüber. der staubige frieden
des feldwegs vorm fenster, ein akkordeon
aus eselsrippen. springt dann und wann
die tür auf, greifen sie mit zittern-
den händen, leise fluchend, nach den karten,
doch spürt man keinen wind. nur ein paar zedern
stehen wie dunkle wolken überm hang.

pinochle

not a shot in years. just those huge mushrooms,
the shadows from the minefields, that grow in dirt
along the border—and the sudden explosions
in early morning, a herd of sheep, dispersed.
from out of the sheets of the calendar,
the alps emerge. a game with three soldiers.

days, nights—with the constellations
of barbed wire above. the dusty calm
of the country road before the window, an accordion
of donkey's ribs. every now and then
the door leaps open: and they reach with tense
hands for the cards, quietly cursing,
yet no one feels the wind. just a few dark cedars
stand above the slope like low-hanging clouds.

nicosia

hinter der grenze schlafen die taxis,
in den geräumten häusern
die sandsäcke, satt vom land.

am frühen abend der muezzin
vom nordteil her, und die biertrinker
des südens, die ihm lauschen, schweigend
auf ihren plastikstühlen, hinter ihnen
der kühlschrank, ein summender weißer gott.

dort, in einer seitenstraße, siehst du
den schneider seine stoffe entrollen
wie ein feldherr seine karten,
während draußen die laternen stich um stich
den abend in die straßen nähen.

dunkler die palmen im park, die bäume;
ab und zu ein wind, der müde
in einer glut von orangen stochert —
und wie im traum die fahrt richtung westen,
an den neubauflächen vorbei, den toten
katzen, flach wie schatten. am rand der straße
bettelt der ginster.

nicosia

behind the border the taxis sleep.
in all the cleared houses
lie sandbags, gorged with the land.

in the twilight sings the muezzin
from the northern part, and the beer drinkers
of the south, who listen to him, silent
on their plastic stools, and behind them
the refrigerator, a humming white god.

there, on a side street, you can see
the tailor rolling open his fabrics
like a field marshal his maps,
while outside the lanterns sew, stitch
by stitch, the evening into the streets.

darker grow the palm leaves in the park, the trees;
now and then comes wind that tiredly
rifles through a glow of oranges—
and driving westward, as in a dream,
the plane of new buildings, the dead
cats flat like shadows. along the shoulder
begs the gorse.

mais

es ist ein feld, in dem du dich verirrst
beim spielen, als der schatten länger fällt,
und hektar oder werst
von feld, von wind, von feld

trennen dich von zuhause.
blätterrascheln — wie das mischen
von karten. später zwischen sternenmassen
ein neues bild: der hakenschlagende hase.

du schläfst, zusammengerollt wie ein tier.
es ist ein morgen, wenn die sonne
dich findet mit vor durst gespalten-

em schädel. über dir
die meterhohen, schwankenden gestalten,
grinsend, das maul voller goldzähne.

corn

in this field you might get lost
playing, as the shadow falls
longer and the acres or miles
of gust, of field, of gust,

separate you from home. rustling
leaves—like the shuffling
of cards. later between masses of stars
a new image: the zigzaggy hare.

you sleep, curled up in silence
like an animal. by morning the sun
finds you, your skull cleaved

with thirst. above you stands
the meters-high, towering outline,
grinning, a jaw crammed with gold teeth.

II

champignons

wir trafen sie im wald auf einer lichtung:
zwei expeditionen durch die dämmerung
die sich stumm betrachteten. zwischen uns nervös
das telegraphensummen des stechmückenschwarms.

meine großmutter war berühmt für ihr rezept
der *champignons farcis*. sie schloß es in
ihr grab. alles was gut ist, sagte sie,
füllt man mit wenig mehr als mit sich selbst.

später in der küche hielten wir
die pilze ans ohr und drehten an den stielen —
wartend auf das leise knacken im innern,
suchend nach der richtigen kombination.

mushrooms

we met them in the forest at a clearing:
two expeditions through the twilight
that mutely watched each other. between us, nervously,
the telegraph hum of a mosquito swarm.

my grandmother was famous for her recipe
of *champignons farcis*. she locked it into
her grave. whatever is good, said she,
one fills with little more than just itself.

later in the kitchen we held the mushrooms
close to our ears and turned the stems—
waiting for the gentle clicking inside,
searching for the proper combination.

historien: onesilos

"Der Leiche des Onesilos schnitten die Amathusier, weil er ihre Stadt belagert hatte, den Kopf ab und nahmen ihn mit nach Amathus, wo sie ihn über dem Stadttor aufhängten. In dem schon ausgehöhlten Schädel setzt sich später ein Bienenschwarm fest und füllte ihn mit Honigwaben."
—HERODOT, *HISTORIEN* V, 114

da oben, der schädel am stadttor,
der mit dem ersten licht zu summen beginnt,
mit dem noch immer leicht verdatter-
ten ausdruck, wo sich ein gesicht befand.

dahinter arbeitet es: die feine
schwarmmechanik im kranium,
die goldenen zahnräder der bienen,
die ineinandergreifen. geranien

und tulpen, wilder mohn und gladiolen —
stück für stück kehrt alles in den blinden
korb zurück, bis in den höhlen
die bienenaugen zu rollen beginnen.

den jungen ist es egal,
wie man ihn nannte, bettler oder könig,
sobald sie über sonnenwarme ziegel
nach oben klettern, der honig,

den er sich ausdenkt, an den händen klebt.
der bienentanz, ein epitaph.
er hatte fast ein land, als er noch lebte.
nun lebt in seinem kopf ein ganzer staat.

histories: onesilos

*"The people of Amathus cut the head from Onesilos' dead body, for he had
besieged the city; they took the head with them to Amathus and hung it high
above the gates. Later a swarm of bees settled in the hollow skull, filling it
with honeycombs."*
—HERODOTUS, *HISTORIES* V, 114

up there: the skull at the city gate
that with the first light starts to hum,
still holds to that slightly agape
expression, where the face had been.

something labors behind it: the del-
icate swarm mechanics in the cranium,
the bees a set of golden cog wheels
that intertwine. geraniums

and tulips, wild poppies, gladiolas—
piecemeal all things return in their ways
to the blind hive, until the bee eyes
in their sockets commence to roll.

for the boys it makes no difference
what name they called him once,
beggar or king, when they scale the
sun-warmed bricks, and the honey

he invents sticks to their fingers.
the bee dance is an epitaph.
he almost had a kingdom while alive.
now, inside his head: this empire.

moorochsen

die dommel sah ich nie, versteckt
im schilf, wie sich das schilf in ihr versteckte,
nie eines ihrer kunstsinnigen nester,
genäht aus licht und schatten, dachte stattdessen

erneut an wriggers' herde,
die eines abends durch ihr gatter
gebrochen war und sich im moor verirrte,
das brüllen, das erst stunden später matter

und mutlos wurde, sich am ende legte,
dachte an all die körper, die versunken
unter dem trügerischen boden schwebten
wie zeppeline, groß und stumm, noch als die jungen

die nester längst verlassen haben mußten,
so daß ich, wenn wir uns am tor versammel-
ten, fröstelnd in das dunkel lauschten, wußte
oder nicht wußte: da, das war sie, die dommel.

moor-oxen

i never saw the bittern in the reeds,
the way the reed had hid itself in her,
i never saw one of her ornate nests,
sewn from light and shadow, and so i began to consider

the wriggers' herds again,
and how, one evening, they trampled over
the wire fence and lost their way,
and i thought of the roar that in just a few hours

had grown faint and discouraged, to fade
at the end, and i thought of the bodies, sunk
in the treacherous ground, how they hovered
like zeppelins, big and mute—even when the chicks

had long since (i imagined) left their nests—
so when we gathered, when i listened
at the gate, shivering into the darkness,
i could almost tell: there, that was her, the bittern.

wippe

mach dich schwerer, rufen sie, also schließe
ich beide augen, denke
an säcke voll zement und eisengieße-
reien, elefanten, an den anker

in seinem schlamm, wo ein manöver wale
vorübergleitet, an das bullenhaupt
eines ambosses. nur eine weile
die luft anhalten, warten. doch nichts hebt

sich oder senkt sich, während ein fasan
schreit und die blätter fallen — meine unwilligen
beine zu kurz, um je den grund zu fassen,
mein kopf beinahe in den wolken.

seesaw

make yourself heavier, they shout,
so i close my eyes, consider
bags full of cement and iron foun-
dries, elephants, and the anchor

in its mud, where a skulk of whales
glides past; consider the bull's head
of an anvil. to hold for just a while
one's breath, wait. but nothing heaves

itself or sinks, while a pheasant
cries out and the leaves fall—my reluctant
legs too short to ever touch the ground,
my head nearly in the clouds.

störtebeker

"Ich bin der neunte, ein schlechter Platz.
Aber noch läuft er."
—GÜNTER EICH

noch läuft er, sieht der kopf dem körper zu
bei seinem vorwärtstaumel. aber wo
ist er, er selbst? in diesen letzten blicken
vom korb her oder in den blinden schritten?
ich bin der neunte, und es ist oktober;
die kälte und das hanfseil schneiden tiefer
ins fleisch. wir knien, aufgereiht, in tupfern
von weiß die wolken über uns, als rupfe
man federvieh dort oben — wie vor festen
die frauen. vater, der mit bleichen fäusten
den stiel umfaßt hielt, und das blanke beil,
das zwinkerte im licht. das huhn derweil
lief blutig, flatternd, seinen weg zu finden
zwischen zwei welten, vorbei an uns johlenden kindern.

störtebeker[1]

"I am the ninth, a bad position.
But still he is walking."
—GÜNTER EICH

still he is walking, the head observing the back
as it reels forward. but where
is he, he himself? in this last look
from the basket or in the blind run?
i am the ninth and it is october;
the cold and the hemp rope cut deeper
into the flesh. we kneel, in a row; in whorls
of white the clouds above us, as if a fowl
hanging, cleaned, like before dinner
when the women would pluck them. father,
who with pale fists held the shaft, and the whetted blade
winked in the light. meanwhile the chicken
ran bloody, flapping, to find his road
between two worlds, past us howling children.

---

1   Klaus Störtebeker, a well-known pirate, was sentenced to death in
     Hamburg in 1402. Before his decapitation he was granted one last wish.
     He wanted to try, after his beheading, to run beyond the fellow prisoners
     lined up before him and the executioner. Any he could pass would be
     pardoned. According to legend, he successfully made it past a few.

giersch

nicht zu unterschätzen: der giersch
mit dem begehren schon im namen — darum
die blüten, die so schwebend weiß sind, keusch
wie ein tyrannentraum.

kehrt stets zurück wie eine alte schuld,
schickt seine kassiber
durchs dunkel unterm rasen, unterm feld,
bis irgendwo erneut ein weißes wider-

standsnest emporschießt. hinter der garage,
beim knirschenden kies, der kirsche: giersch
als schäumen, als gischt, der ohne ein geräusch

geschieht, bis hoch zum giebel kriecht, bis giersch
schier überall sprießt, im ganzen garten giersch
sich über giersch schiebt, ihn verschlingt mit nichts als giersch.

clover

not to underestimate:
clover, with the cleaving in its name.
thus the flower, white, the petals cloven, chaste
as a tyrant's dream.

it comes back always like a debt unpaid
and sends its correspondence
in secret, through the darkness underground, under the field,
until a clever white resistance

cell erupts. behind the car park,
by the crunching gravel, the ficus tree: clover,
as ocean, as sea foam, how wavelike

it crashes, becoming froth, until clover
very nearly captures everything, as in the whole copse clover
covers over clover, culling until all is gone but clover.

laken

großvater wurde einbalsamiert
in seines und hinausgetragen,
und ich entdeckte ihn ein jahr später,
als wir die betten frisch bezogen,
zur wespe verschrumpelt, winziger
pharao eines längst vergangenen sommers.

so faltete man laken: die arme
weit ausgebreitet, daß man sich zu spiegeln
begann über die straffgespannte fläche
hinweg; der wäschefoxtrott dann, bis schritt
um schritt ein rechteck im nächstkleineren
verschwand, bis sich die nasen fast berührten.

alles konnte verborgen sein
in ihrem schneeigen innern: ein leerer
flakon mit einem spuk parfum, ein paar
lavendelblüten oder wiesenblumen,
ein groschen oder ab und zu ein wurf
von mottenkugeln in seinem nest.

fürs erste aber ruhten sie, stumm
und weiß in ihren schränken, ganze
stapel von ihnen, eingelegt in duft,
gemangelt, gebügelt, gestärkt,
und sorgfältig gepackt wie fallschirme
vor einem sprung aus ungeahnten höhen.

bedsheets

grandfather was embalmed
in his, and carried out,
and once, a year later, when i was making that bed,
i discovered him again,
shriveled to a wasp, minuscule
pharaoh of a bygone summer.

we folded sheets this way: the arms
made wide until your mirror self
would bring the tight-stretched surface
across. a linen fox-trot followed, and step
after step of increasingly smaller rectangles,
each vanishing, till your noses almost touched.

everything could be hidden
in their snowy interior: an empty
flacon with a haunting of perfume, a few
lavender blossoms or field flowers,
a dime, or now and again a litter
of mothballs in its nest.

for now, however, they rested, mute
and white in their cabinets, whole
piles of them, pickled in fragrance,
mangled, ironed, starched, and carefully
packed like parachutes
before a jump from unforeseen heights.

im brunnen

sechs, sieben meter freier fall
und ich war weiter weg
als je zuvor, ein kosmonaut
in seiner kapsel aus feldstein,
betrachtete aus der ferne
das kostbare, runde blau.

ich war das kind
im brunnen. nur die moose
kletterten am geflochtenen
strick ihrer selbst nach oben,
efeu stieg über efeuschultern
ins freie, entkam.

ab und zu der weiße blitz
eines vogels, ab und zu
der weiße vogel blitz. ich aß,
was langsamer war. der mond,
der sich über die öffnung schob,
ein forscherauge überm mikroskop.

gerade, als ich die wörter assel und stein
als assel und stein zu begreifen lernte,
drang lärm herab, ein hasten, schreie,
und vor mir begann ein seil.

ich kehrte zurück ins läuten der glocken,
zurück zu brotgeruch und busfahrplänen,
dem schatten unter bäumen,

in the well

six, seven meters free fall
and i was farther away
than ever before, a cosmonaut
in his space capsule of fieldstone,
observing from the distance
the precious, round blue.

i was the child
in the well. only the mosses
climbed on the braided
rope of themselves upward,
and ivy clambered over ivy shoulders
into the free, escaping.

now and then the white bolt
of a bird, now and then
the white bird bolt. i ate
what was slower than me. the moon
slid over the opening,
a researcher eye above the microscope.

just as i began to grasp
the words bug, and stone
as bug, and stone,
there interceded noise, a hastening, shouts,
and in front of me appeared a rope.

i returned into the tolling of the bells,
back to bread smell and bus schedules,
the shadow under trees,

gesprächen übers wetter, kehrte
zurück zu taufen und tragödien,
den schlagzeilen, von denen
ich eine war.

conversations about weather, returned
back to baptisms and tragedies,
the headlines, one of which
i was.

selbstporträt mit bienenschwarm

bis eben nichts als eine feine linie
um kinn und lippen, jetzt ein ganzer bart,
der wächst und wimmelt, bis ich magdalena
zu gleichen scheine, ganz und gar behaart

von bienen bin. wie es von allen seiten
heranstürmt, wie man langsam, gramm um gramm
an dasein zunimmt, an gewicht und weite,
das regungslose zentrum vom gesang . . .

ich ähnele mit meinen ausgestreck-
ten armen einem ritter, dem die knappen
in seine rüstung helfen, stück um stück,
erst helm, dann harnisch, arme, beine, nacken,

bis er sich kaum noch rühren kann, nicht läuft,
nur schimmernd dasteht, nur mit ein paar winden
hinter dem glanz, ein bißchen alter luft,
und wirklich sichtbar erst mit dem verschwinden.

self-portrait with a swarm of bees

until just now there had been nothing but a line
around the chin and lips, but then a proper beard
that grows and teems, until i look like magdalene
in her ascension, wound round and round with hair

made of a swarm of bees. from every angle how it storms
into this center, how i slowly gain, gram after gram,
in being, how i increase in weight and vastness,
become the crux of singing, motionless . . .

and i stand here with arms stretched out-
ward like a knight, whom the knaves
help into his armor, plate after plate,
first helmet, then harness, arms, legs, nape,

until no force could budge him, who does not move,
but stands here shimmering, with what blows
behind this splendor, a bit of old air, and is perceived
only at the point he disappears.

lazarus

vier tage nur, dann kehrte er zurück,
erst blind wie eine kartoffel, etwas moder
um bart und haare, kroch aus seinem sarg,
einer hölzernen mutter,

und war noch gegen den wind zu riechen.
er schien zu lauschen, ob sein herz noch schlug,
sobald er saß; versteckt hinter den röcken
die kinder, wenn er um die ecke bog,

als würde er weder dem boden trauen
noch seinem eigenen, tastenden schritt.
wir sahen seine frau mit roten augen.
die beiden schliefen jetzt zu dritt.

vier wochen, bis man nicht länger meinte,
im schinken die erde zu schmecken, den lehm
in wasser oder wein; vier monate,
und alles blasser, alles wundersam

und fast schon vergessen —
da steht er plötzlich hinten in der schlange
um brot an, hört man im dunkel der gassen
erneut diese schnarrende feder von stimme,

als ob etwas in ihm zerris-
sen ist, spricht ihn mit "guten abend" an
vielleicht, mit "schönes wetter, lazarus,"
und streckt die hand aus, hält den atem an.

lazarus

he only had four days, then he returned.
blind at first like a potato, moldier
around the beard and hair, he squirmed
out of his coffin, his wooden mother,

and i could smell him even upwind.
he was listening to whether the heart still pounded,
whenever he sat down. our children hid
in skirts of women when he rounded

corners. he trusted not the ground,
nor even his own clumsy, fumbling feet.
i watched the eyes of the wife go red.
the two of them now slept as three.

then i thought about things less, the earth
in ham, four weeks gone by; and the loam
in water and wine, fading; four months
and all much paler now; all wonders soon

forgotten—until, quite suddenly,
say, i see him waiting in the line
for bread, or, this instant, when i hear in the alley
that stammering whir of his voice again,

like for the first time—as if it tears
itself apart in him—when i greet him,
"good evening" or "fine weather, lazarus,"
extending my hand, nobody breathing.

amisch

was wir für eine schwarze kutsche hielten,
war nur der schatten einer wolke, saß
als schwarm von raben über einem aas,
bis wir die schwarze kutsche überholten.

die scheunen zwischen tag und nacht, die farmen,
von wäsche blind; das rübenstecken,
das sticken, und wie riesige insekten-
eier die wassertürme in der ferne.

der laden führte bottiche, propan-
gaslampen, einen fahnensaal von sensen.
amanda kaufte eine dieser puppen

ohne gesicht, als prompt zwei pferdebremsen
sich niederließen, ein paar dunkle augen,
die schielten, krabbelten, dann weiterflogen.

amish

what we assumed was a black carriage
was really shadows from a cloud, now changed
to a murder of crows on some carrion they savaged,
until we passed it by: now, a black carriage.

their barns that witnessed evenings, mornings,
and farms, blinded by laundry;
the planting of turnips; their embroidery;
and distant water towers like the eggs

of huge insects. the general store stocked
tubs, propane lanterns, a flag hall of scythes.
amanda bought one of those dolls, it was a sock

without a face, when promptly two horseflies
landed, a black, squinting pair of eyes
that briefly crawled and then flew off again.

elegie für knievel

"God, take care of me — here I come . . ."

die landschaft zog schlieren, sobald sie ihn sah.
ein draufgänger, ein teufelskerl
mit einem hemd voller sterne
und stets verfolgt von dem hornissenschwarm
des motorenlärms. die knochen brachen,
die knochen wuchsen zusammen, und er sprang.

wieviele hindernisse zwischen rampe
und jenem fernen punkt?
wieviele ausrangierte doppeldecker?
was war ihm der zweifel, der sich eingräbt
im innern, bis ein ganzer cañon klafft
mit rieselndem sand an den rändern,
den schreien großer vögel?

nachmittage, an denen sich die geschichte
für einen augenblick niederließ,
um nach popcorn und abgas zu duften.
wie hier, in yakima, washington,
mit diesem zerbeulten mond überm stadion
und tausenden, denen der atem stockt:
fünfzehn, zwanzig busse und das rad
steht in der luft.

elegy for knievel

"God, take care of me—here I come . . ."

wherever it saw him, the land began to blur.
this daredevil, this hotshot,
his shirt full of stars
and ever pursued by the hornet swarm
of engine noise. the bones broke,
the bones coalesced, and he jumped.

how many obstacles between the ramp
and that distant point?
how many discarded double-deckers?
what doubts did he have, the kind that sink
to the interior, until a whole canyon gapes
with trickling sand at its edges
and the cries of huge birds?

afternoons, when history
fell still for a moment,
fragrant as popcorn and exhaust.
like here, in yakima, washington,
this dented moon above the stadium
and the thousands whose breath is caught:
fifteen, twenty buses, and his wheels
in the air.

austern

ich bin nur der, der general junot am morgen
sein frühstück bringt, wenn *plate* und *creuse*
wie seltsame orden
in einer schale liegen, die karosse

der wolken über uns aufs neue
ins rollen gerät — dreihundert ißt er,
selbst jetzt, selbst hier auf diesem hügel in der nähe
von auster-, auster-, auster-

litz: ein leichter duft von pulver-
dampf hing überm land,
als ich hinabstieg, um trompetenpfiffer-
linge und holz zu sammeln (hinter mir in einem schrank

aus schnee ein dutzend flaschen muscadet
zum kühlen), und an einem teich im forst
den reiher bemerkte, steif wie ein kadett
und ohne jede angst — bis ich ihn fast

berühren konnte, sah, daß nur die schicht
aus eis den toten vogel stützte.
als ich zurückkam, war die schlacht
vorüber, die geschütze

verstummt. vorm zelt der große haufen
leerer schalen, ihr geruch von weite
und fäulnis. boten liefen
durchs lager, um die nachricht zu verbreiten.

oysters
   austerlitz

mornings i alone bring general junot
his breakfast, when *plate* and *creuse*
like unseemly medals of honor
lie in a bowl, the caroche

of the overhung clouds once more
getting started to roll—three hundred
he eats, even now, even here on this mound
near oyster, oyster-, auster-

litz: a light scent of gunpowder
was hanging across the land, as i alone
went down to collect the trumpet chanter-
elles and wood (behind me in the trunk

of snow a dozen bottles of muscadet
to chill), and noticed a heron at the pond
in the forest, stiff as a young cadet
and devoid of any fear—until i could

almost touch him, then discovered
that only a layer of ice supported
the dead bird. when i returned,
the battle was over, the rifle reports

silenced. in front of the tent was the heap
of used shells, their odor of vastness
and decay. messengers across the camp
were already spreading the news.

patience

ich sehe es noch. im busch die zwei versteckten
räder und das waldlicht, der talon,
nach dem die farnhand greift, die decke
mit ihren plastiktellern,

den überresten vom baiser.
im schilf die allianz von wasserläufern.
libellen kontrollieren die pässe
der mückenlarven.

man könnte gerade noch zu uns hinüberrufen
durch diesen sommer, den geruch von modder,
der fremd und schlüpfrig über allem steht,

ein gutes stück vom ufer
entfernt, wie bube und dame in der mitte
gespiegelt, bis zum nabel schon im see.

solitaire

i can still see it. behind the bush
the two hidden bikes and the forest light,
the stack of cards, the fern's reach,
the blanket with its paper plates,

what's left of the rich cherry pie.
in the reeds an alliance of water striders.
dragonflies checkpoint the progress
of mosquito larvae.

someone could just call across to us
through this summer, the scent of mud
that rises above everything, slick and primordial,

a fair length away from the shores,
like the jack and queen, mirrored
at the center of the lake, above the navel.

der mann aus dem meer

man findet ihn in einem frack aus salz
und sand. ein paß aus algen, ein ensemble
von heringsmöwen hinter ihm. der nebel.

er spricht nicht, dafür läßt er am klavier die filz-
brandung hüpfen, durchs gehäuse wogen,
daß man erstaunt. die schweren epauletten
der hände, die sich auf die schultern legen;
die stunde ruhm, die ära der tabletten,

die nächte im herbst: auf den gängen treiben die pfleger
wie eisberge vorüber. in dem klinik-
garten unter den mauern ein geflacker
letzter blätter, aus dem alten schuppen,
an dem der efeu steigt, gedämpftes klingen
eines klaviers. man hält es für chopin.

the man from the sea

you find him dressed in coattails: salt
and sand. green passport of algae.
ensemble of black-backed gulls. the fog.

he doesn't speak. instead he lets the felt-
hammers roil in the piano case,
astounding you. the heavy epaulets
of hands which lie atop the shoulders;
the hour in glory, the era of tablets,

the autumn nights: through corridors the nurses
pass like icebergs. in the clinic
beneath the garden walls, a shuddering
of late leaves, and coming from the shed
on which the ivy rises, a muffled tune
from the piano. you take it for chopin.

dobermann

für Ron Winkler

dies ist das dorf, und dies am waldesrand
die wasenmeisterei, von deren dach
ein dünner rauch sich in den himmel stiehlt.

die leeren felle an der wand. der korb
mit welpen, ihre augen noch vernäht
von blindheit: so beschnüffeln sie die welt.

noch ist es früh, und in den städten schlafen
die landvermesser und die kartographen.
im garten jener brunnen voller durst.

apolda, thüringen: die tote kuh
am feldrand, ein gestrandeter ballon,
von seuche aufgebläht. sie wird

dort liegen bleiben: unter einem kleingeld
von sternen schreitet er, an dessen seite
zwei schwarze klingen durch die landschaft schneiden.

doberman

for Ron Winkler

this is the village, and at the edge of woods
the knacker's yard, from whose roof
a plume of smoke steals into the sky.

the empty skins, hung on the wall. the basket
of puppies, their eyes stitched tight
in blindness: so they snuffle up the world.

yet it is early, and in the cities sleep
the land surveyor and cartographer.
in the garden is the well, filled with thirst.

apolda, in thuringia: the dead cow
on the field's edge, a stranded balloon,
bloated by plague. it is

to remain here: beneath the pocket change
of stars, he strides, as on each side of him
the two black blades keep cutting through the land.

der wassermann

für Robin Robertson

einer zog mich mit dem ersten fang
vor husum an bord, den obolus
einer muschel in der heilbuttkalten hand,
um mich herum der silberne applaus

der heringe auf dem deck. ihr heißer grog
verbrannte mich bis auf die gräten,
an anderes gewöhnte ich mich: die glock-
en jeden sonntag. schnee. an federbetten.

man fand den eifersüchtigen bauerntrampel
ertrunken in einer pfütze. eine saat
ging auf. als eines morgens der vergammel-
te dorsch vor meiner tür lag, war es zeit.

ich hinterließ die angst der schlafenden
vorm wasser, eine fußspur, die die sonne
bald auflecken würde, und die gaffenden
nachbarn um mütter und wiegen, ihre söhne

mit fischlippen und schwimmhaut. ohne eile
sank ich zurück zu dem mit flunderaugen ausgelegten
palast, wo meine frau mit ihrer mühle
das salz ins meer dreht. ich wurde meine legende.

the merman

for Robin Robertson

before husum, with the first catch
they pulled me on board, the obolus
of a shell in my hand, cold as halibut,
the herring and their silver applause

surrounding me on deck. their hot grog
burnt me down to the fish ribs,
but i got used to other things: to the clock
and its bells. to snow. to featherbeds.

they found the yokel, the jealous one,
drowned in a puddle. a seed
arose. one morning when the cod
lay rotting at my door, i took that as a sign.

i left behind the angst of the sleeping,
who fear water in their dreams, my prints
licked away by the sun, and i left the gaping
neighbors, the mothers and their prams,

their sons with fish lips and webs.
unhurried i sank back down to the palace,
its walls of flounder eyes, where my wife
grinds salt for the sea. i became my own myth.

steinway

der schwarze flügel, den die männer
über die straße hievten,
war der vereiste see aus meiner
kindheit, wo ich kniete,

um durch die blanke fläche
hinabzustarren,
wo zwischen algen und kristall die hechte
für einen augenblick verharrten,

in ihrem dunkel hingen,
jeder eine schimmernde fermate
in einer bis zum knochen dringen-
den urmusik, in ihrer mathe-

matischen, tödlich präzisen
schönheit, für die sekunde,
die wächst, bis sie so groß zu sein
scheint, daß man in ihr siedeln könnte,

weit weg vom weg, vom stein
darauf,
und fast schon festgefroren mit der stirn,
als der puck mich traf.

steinway

the grand piano the men
heaved across the street
became the frozen pond
of my childhood, where i knelt

against the bare surface
and straight down gazed
there between algae and ice
where pike lurked,

hung in their shadows,
each one a shining fermata
in an ur-music
that penetrates bone, with mathe-

matical, deadly accurate
beauty, swelling for a moment
until it grows so giant
you might live inside it,

far from the road, from the
stone surfaces of things, the pond
frozen, almost, to my forehead,
as the puck hit me.

schlehen

was war so blau wie abende im herbst
oder schwarz wie die bibel? hing durch nebelschleier,
oktoberschauer, war so herbe, herbst,
daß alles sich zusammenzog? die schlehe.

wir zogen ihnen nach dem ersten frost
am waldrand entgegen: busch um busch barbaren,
verschanzt hinter den dornen — und vereist
der boden, wo wir knieten, nach den beeren

zu tasten, ihrer zarten und damas-
tenen haut, um vorsichtig hineinzugreifen,
zu suchen wie der ungläubige thomas
im wundmal. zeit genug, um abzuschweifen,

an anderes zu denken — an osmose,
die nächste klassenarbeit, nylonstrümpfe,
an nina wriggers' brüste und den kosmos,
der irgendwann in naher zukunft seine
 grenze, jenen punkt der größtmöglichen
 ausdehnung erreichen und zu schrumpfen

beginnen würde, himmel, länder, schule
und stadt, wir selber, bis die ganze welt
von nichts als einem zweiglein hinge: schlehe.
kein wunder, wie schwer die eimer waren, gefüllt

mit tiefster bläue. hinter uns die sträucher —
ein text, fast ganz befreit von den vokalen,
ein dickicht, ein paar wirre federstriche.
die reste überließen wir den vögeln.

sloes

what was so blue like evenings in the fall
or black like the bible? what hung, was so harsh,
through mist smoke, october showers, so whol-
ly bitter that everything contracted? the sloe.

we moved toward them after the first frost
at the forest edge—in-the-rough barbarians,
entrenched behind the thorns, and iced
on the ground, where we kneeled for the berries

to grope for their tender and damas-
ked skin, to cautiously grasp at the interior,
to search the inside like a doubting thomas
asks questions, and there was time to wonder,

to think of other things—of osmosis,
the next class test, nylon stockings,
of nina wriggers's breasts and of the cosmos,
which at some point in the nearing future
        would reach its border, its point of greatest
        possible extension, and start to shrink

starting with the sky, with the country, school,
and city, with us ourselves, until the whole world
upon nothing but a twiglet would hang: sloe.
no wonder, how heavy the buckets were, filled

with deepest blue. behind us the bushes—
a text, almost devoid of vowels, its words
a thicket, a bunch of tangled pen scratches.
the rest of it we left there to the birds.

kentaurenblues

wir haben helden vergiftet, prinzen gelehrt,
haben helden vergiftet, faß um faß geleert,
und doch war alles irgendwie verkehrt.

wo hört das roß auf, wo beginnt der reiter?
wer weiß schon, ob er roß ist oder reiter?
etwas hielt inne. etwas galoppierte weiter.

die mutter, eine wolke, die uns aufzog,
bis jene düsterere wolke aufzog,
unter den fesseln durch die wiesen flog —

und wir, berauscht vom raub, mit dampfendem fell,
ein lärm in den wäldern. heute dampft kein fell,
klappert kein huf mehr, und die nacht ist grell.

wenn du am fluß stehst aber, suche im dunst
nach den vertrauten schemen. rechne mit uns.

centaurs' blues

we have poisoned all the heroes, taught princes and their heirs,
we have poisoned all the heroes, got drunk and put on airs,
and all was ruined anyway and made unfair.

where does the rider start? where does the steed end?
who can know if he is steed or rider in the end?
something paused—and something galloped, gathering speed.

our mother was a cloud, she watched us grow up together.
until some darker clouds began to gather,
speeding between our legs through grass and heather,

and us, confused with plunder, with steaming animal skins,
making a racket in forests back then. no steaming skins,
no clatter now of hooves. and the night is blinding.

but if you stand at the river: search through the mist
for our familiar shapes. trust we still exist.

versuch über seife

ein stück war immer in der nähe,
folgte seinen eigenen phasen,
wurde weniger wie fast alles,
stand dann wieder voll
und leuchtend weiß in seiner schale.

wog wie ein stein in der faust,
schäumte auf, wurde weicher:
man wusch sich von kain zu abel.

einmal vergessen, verwitterte sie
zum rissigen asteroidensplitter,
doch ruht jetzt feucht und glänzend
wie etwas, das vom grund des sees
heraufgetaucht wird, sekundenlang kostbar,

und alle sitzen wir am tisch:
mondloser abend, duftende hände.

essay on soap

one piece was always nearby,
followed its own phases,
diminishing like almost everything does;
then stood again full
and luminously white in its bowl.

weighed like a stone in the fist,
in a froth, it became softer:
one washed oneself from cain into abel.

once it was forgotten, it weathered
into a fissured asteroid splinter,
but rests now moist and shiny
like something from the bottom of the lake
that's been quarried, precious for those seconds,

and we have gathered at the table:
moonless evening, fragrant hands.

III

eule

"Schwebe ohne eile, Eule,
Durchs dunkel, deine aula, Eule,
Für dich und mich, uns alle, Eule . . ."

still wie eine urne — bis die rufe
hoch über den köpfen
uns stocken lassen, sonderbar, als rufe
etwas durch sie hindurch; im braunen oder kupfern-

en federkleid zwischen den zweigen sitzend,
mit einem weißen schleier, zart wie mehltau
und brüsseler spitze,
verstreut sie die grazilen amulette

ihrer gewölle,
kaum mehr zu sehen, eher noch zu spüren;
der schlußstein in dem großen laubgewölbe;

ein gelber spalt und noch ein gelber spalt,
zwei augen hinter den tapetentüren
aus borke, dann der wald. der wald. der wald.

owl

"Glide for a while, Owl,
Through gloom, your hall, Owl,
For me and you, for all, Owl . . ."

silent like an urn—until her calls
high above us
cause us to pause, how strange, as if there called
something right through her; in a brown or rust-

colored plumage between the branches,
with a white veil, delicate like mildew
and brussels lace,
she scatters the brittle jewels

of her pellets,
now hardly visible, and rather to be sensed;
the keystone in the giant foliage vault;

a yellow slit, another yellow slit,
two eyes behind the hidden entrance
of bark, and then the woods. the woods. the woods.

aus der globusmanufaktur

einmal verlegte ich mein pausenbrot
in einer südhalbkugel, die noch einzeln
und offen war. nun träumt ein junge, bohrt
sich in der nase, sucht die sandwich-inseln.

eine perfekte welt: mit farben, zonen
und einem herz aus vierzig watt im mittel-
punkt; keine kriege, keine sezessionen,
nur der dezente duft von lösungsmittel.

am abend lassen uns die laster
allein in der halle, tragen in leichten
kartons ihr universum in die fenster
der kinder, jenes runde, blaue leuchten;

wir aber treffen uns am nächsten morgen
im ewigen neon wieder, einer als atlas,
der andere als sonnenfinsternis, demiurgen
im kittel, gottheiten mit latz.

im schlaf erscheint mir der äquator regel-
mäßig als linie, der man folgen könnte
durch wälder, länder, kontinente,
als eine klare grenze: jeder vogel

ist zwei vögel, einer vor
und einer hinter ihm, alles ist immer
exakt getrennt, der tag von nacht, der nor-
den von dem süden. winter starrt auf sommer.

from the globe factory

once, i set down my breaktime bread
in the yet-to-be-constructed portions
of the southern hemisphere. some child
now picks his nose there, seeking the sandwich islands.

it was a perfect world. with colors, zones,
and forty watts as center point;
no wars and no secessions,
only the slight odor of dissolvent.

at night the trucks abandon us to silence
in the hall, and they deliver in light cartons
the cosmos to the windows of the children,
that round, blue radiance;

we however earn the next day's wages
in eternal neon again, one as atlas,
another as a solar eclipse, demiurges
in work coats, deities with overalls.

it's often that i dream of the equator
as a line which one could follow
through the forests, continents, low-
lands, a precise frontier: every bird

becomes two birds, one before
and one behind the line, all things there
are segregated, day from night, north
from south. winter stares at summer.

jede wolke ist zwei wolken, ein schnee-
ball landet als pfütze. das gebirge stockt,
wird ebene, der kleine see
verliert den namen. linkerhand steigt

der rauch vom bäcker auf, rechts wetzt
ein schlachter die messer — und die liebenden winken
sich einmal noch zu, als er sein haus verläßt
und sich bei ihr die jalousien senken.

every cloud is two clouds, a snow-
ball lands as a puddle. the mountainside
halts, becomes a plain, the tiny pond
loses its name. on the left rises smoke

from the baker's, on the right the butcher
whets the knives—and the lovers
wave once more to each other, as he goes
from his house, and at hers the shutters close.

koalas

so viel schlaf in nur einem baum,
so viele kugeln aus fell
in all den astgabeln, eine boheme
der trägheit, die sich in den wipfeln hält und hält

und hält mit ein paar klettereisen
als krallen, nie gerühmte erstbesteiger
über den flötenden terrassen
von regenwald, zerzauste stoiker,

verlauste buddhas, zäher als das gift,
das in den blättern wächst, mit ihren watte-
ohren gegen lockungen gefeit
in einem winkelchen von welt: kein water-

loo für sie, kein gang nach canossa.
betrachte, präge sie dir ein, bevor es
zu spät ist — dieses sanfte knauser-
gesicht, die miene eines radrennfahrers

kurz vorm etappensieg, dem grund entrückt,
und doch zum greifen nah ihr abgelebtes
grau —, bevor ein jeder wieder gähnt, sich streckt,
versinkt in einem traum aus eukalyptus.

koalas

so much sleep in only one tree,
so many gray globes
of fur in all the branches, a bohemia
of sluggishness which itself in the treetops holds and holds

and holds with a couple of crampons
as claws. nor was it ever credited, first to take
the journey above the whistling fans
of rainforest canopy, ruffled stoics,

shoddy buddhas, tougher than the poison
in the leaves, with their cotton wool
ears against enticements, immune
in some cranny of the world: no waterloo

for them, no walk to canossa.
take note of them, memorize them
while there is time—this face in repose,
this expression of a cyclist

very close to stage win, dis-
connected from the ground, but within our reach
in jaded gray, before each of them yawns, stretches,
drops off into a dream of eucalyptus.

krynica morska

wodka aus fünf ländern, in sieben bleichen
bäuchen schwankend, glucksend, andrzej. wir setzten
rundum an und hoben die flaschen: eine
    wodkafanfare.

nacht, die wie ein fesselballon an ihren
regenseilen riß; ein augustgewitter
zog von norden über die see, zog bis nach
    krynica morska,

bis zum strand, rimantas, den kleiderbündeln,
abgelegt zu friedlichen tieren: jeder
blitz riß uns das dunkel vom leib, wir standen
    nackt wie ein stamm da,

eben erst entdeckt. und wir rannten, ilya,
schlugen wellen hinter uns zu und trieben
zwischen schwarz und schwärzer, halina, mikhel,
    schmuggelten all das

hochprozentige durch die brandung, während
uns im rücken, unter dem kettenlicht, die
massenschlägerei in der bar poseidon
    ohne uns anfing.

krynica morska

vodka from five countries, in seven pallid
bellies swaying, gurgling, andrzej. we passed it
all around the room and we raised the bottles:
    vodka as fanfare.

night: a moored balloon which at its rain ropes
tore; an august thunderstorm that trekked from
way up north and over the sea, and trekked to
    krynica morska,

to the beach, rimantas, and to the clothes heaps,
tossed to peaceful animals: every lightning
strike ripped darkness off us, and so we stood there
    naked as a tribe,

only now discovered. and we ran, ilya,
slammed the waves behind us, and we drifted
there between the black and blacker, halina,
    mikhel, and smuggled

all that high-grade stuff through surf, just as
concurrently, beneath the lights all tinkling,
the free-for-all back in the bar poseidon
    began without us.

versuch über servietten

als kühler origamikranich,
oder mit dem stolz von viermastern
über die tische kreuzend,

immer nach norden, nach norden . . .
früh genug fällt ein letztes licht
durch hohé fenster, brennt sich

als soßenfleck in ihr weiß,
liegen sie zerknüllt am tellerrand,
mit nichts als dem roten falter

aus lippenstift im innern; früh genug
'schweben sie mit ihresgleichen
durchs fegefeuer der großwäscherei,

nicht wissend, wozu sie am morgen
auferstehen unter den flinken
händen der kellnerinnen: wird es

ein tänzchen, den belagerten voraus,
die schönheit einer kapitulation?
der späte trick eines betrunkenen,

ein schlüssel, der verschwindet? oder
das lästige summen, jener druckfehler
von fliege im tischtuch, ihr kleines, verschmiertes F?

essay on napkins

as a cool origami crane,
or with the pride of four-masters
tacking over tabletops

always toward the north, the north . . .
soon enough a last light falls
through high windows, burns itself

as a gravy stain into their white;
soon enough they lie upended at the rim
of the plate, nothing but the red butterfly

of lipstick inside; and they float
with others of their ilk through
the purgatory fire of the industrial laundry,

not knowing into what
they will resurrect under the nimble
hands of the waitresses: will it be

a miniscule dance, preceding the siege,
the beauty of a surrender?
the late trick of a drunkard

to make a key disappear? or will it be
the irritating buzz, that typo
of a fly in the tablecloth, its tiny, blotted F?

nagel

kaum in der wand, war er die mitte,
schnellte sein radius
über die gärten, felder, rübenmiete
hinaus, die hühnerställe, das radies-

chenbeet, wurde umfassender, mondial:
wir hängten die hüte auf. wir hängten strick-
jacken und rahmen, hängten regenmäntel
und schirme auf, bis wir ihn fast vergaßen, dessen harter blick

noch da sein wird, wenn wir längst ausgezogen
und stadt und haus und straße
verschwunden sind — so unbeirrt weit oben,

so glänzend über west und ost,
daß sich im dunkeln navigieren ließe
nach ihm, und alten seefahrern ein trost.

nail

scarcely in the wall, he was the center,
expanding its radius
across the gardens, fields, beet briar,
and farther, to the henhouses, the radish

patch, becoming more worldy, all-encompassing:
we hung up the hats. we hung up cardigans
and picture frames, hung coats, umbrellas,
until we almost forgot him, whose hard gaze

will still be there, when we have long since moved away
and house and street and town
have vanished—so undeterredly

far, so lustrous, so above the east and west
that one could navigate through darkness
by him, offering old sailors consolation.

regentonnenvariationen

ich hob den deckel
und blickte ins riesige
auge der amsel.

*

unterm pflaumenbaum
hinterm haus — gelassen, kühl
wie ein zenmeister.

*

eine art ofen
im negativ; qualmte nicht,
schluckte die wolken.

*

gluckste nur kurz auf,
trat man zornig dagegen,
aber gab nichts preis.

*

als stiege durch sie
die unterwelt hinauf, um
uns zu belauschen.

rain barrel variations

i lifted the lid
and stared into the giant
eye of the blackbird.

*

beneath the plum tree
behind the house, unmoved, cool
like a zen master.

*

a sort of oven
in negative, without smoke,
gulping up the clouds.

*

gurgled just a bit,
if you bashed hard against it,
but disclosed nothing.

*

as if the dead climbed
through her from the netherworld,
to listen to us.

*

silberne orgel-
pfeife, fallrohr: dort hindurch
pumpte das wetter.

*

einen sommer lang
ganz versunken. dann, bei sturm,
schäumte sie über.

*

bleib, sprach das dunkel,
und dein gesicht löst sich auf
wie ein stück zucker.

*

alt wie der garten,
duftend wie ein waldsee. stand
da, ein barrel styx.

*

ich hob den deckel,
zuckte zurück. der amsel-
gesang dunkelte.

*

silvery organ
pipe, squat gutter spout: through which
pumped all the weather.

*

one summer long
fully sated. then, with storm,
it bubbled over.

*

stay, spoke that darkness,
and your face dissolves itself
like a sugar lump.

*

old as the garden,
redolent as forest-lake.
there: barrel of styx.

*

i lifted the lid,
twitched back. the blackbird singing
suddenly darkened.

*

übervoll im herbst,
lief sie aus in hunderten
schwarzer nacktschnecken.

*

was ich im kopf be-
hielt, eingefaßt vom rund: das
medaillon „ratte".

*

ein letzter tropfen
vom baum. in der stille, still,
der bebende gong.

*

ein grübeln, grübeln;
im winter die erleuchtung
als scheibe von eis.

＊

awash in autumn,
it leaked out by the hundreds
the heaps of black slugs.

＊

what got imprinted
in me, framed in the barrel,
like a locket: *rat.*

＊

last drop from the tree.
in the quiet, quietly,
the quivering gong.

＊

a brooding, brooding;
in winter, enlightenment
as a disc of ice.

versuch über zäune

manchmal klaffte ein loch im draht,
    als hätte sich ein satellit
    zu nah an die erde gewagt, aus sehnsucht
    nach gräsern, nach dem roten tulpenfunk,

oder eine weiße planke hing
    so lose, daß man sie ziehen konnte,
    durchs grinsen eines vagabunden
    in aufgeräumte gärten stieg.

alles begann ja erst hinter ihnen,
    das ahnten wir, wenn sie uns lautlos folgten,
    durch wiesen, elektrisch vom grillensommer,
    vorbei an koppeln, am wippenden korn;

auf ihren warmen rücken zu sitzen,
    mit rittersporn am fuß und einem pulk
    von brennesseln im gefolge, hier
    ein wimpel gelber wolle, dort

am holz der prachtvolle doppelmond
    eines ackergauls, und hin und wieder einer,
    der unbezwingbar blieb — nur das gespenst
    des löwenzahns zog mühelos hindurch.

wo die große straße abbog,
    trennten wir uns. aus einigen wurden diebe,
    aus anderen kirschbäume. oh, die amsel glühte,
    wenn wir am abend in den betten lagen.

essay on fences

sometimes there gaped a hole in the chain,
    as if a satellite
    had snuck too close to earth, longing
    for grasses, for the radio waves of red tulip.

or sometimes a white picket hung
    so loose that you could pull it out,
    becoming the smirk of a vagabond
    through which we'd enter tidied gardens.

everything began behind them,
    that much we could see, when they followed us quietly
    through meadows, electric from cricket summers,
    past all the paddocks, the teetering grain;

and to lean against their warm backs
    with larkspur at the foot and a throng
    of stinging nettles as entourage, here
    a yellow wool pennant, there

against the board the great double moon
    of a plowhorse's haunches, and now and again one fence
    that remained unscalable—only the ghost
    of a dandelion gliding effortlessly through.

where the great road took a turn,
    we went our separate ways. some became
    cherry thieves. others cherry trees. oh the blackbird
    called, when we lay in our beds at night.

elch

der warme doppellauf wie eine schlag-
ader in meiner faust. ein kurzer knall
und schon vorüber, während noch von tal
zu tal das leuchtfeuer des echos jagt.

um mich versammelt ragt die stumme runde
von onkeln auf. die bärte, eingeflochten
die perlen aus eis darin; das rinnende
wasser unter schneebedeckten schluchten.

wir folgen seiner blutspur um den buckel
des hügels. übelkeit, ein spätes licht —
dann seine schaufeln, um die luft gelegt
wie hände eines champions am pokal.

elk

the warm double-barrel like an art-
ery in my fist. a sudden blast
and it's already over, while still from forest
to forest the beacon of the echo blazes outward.

gathered around me, the mute round
of uncles stand up: the beards, wrung
with pearls of ice within them; beneath mount-
ains covered in snow, water is streaming.

around the foothill's hunchback we follow the blood.
sick to my stomach, a very late light—
then his antlers clenching at the air
like the champion's hands at the prize cup.

ficus watkinsiana

beginnt, wo andere aufhören wollen,
    im licht; seilt sich ab aus sich selbst,
    trifft exakt jenes winzige öhr
    im regenwald, fädelt sich ein.

entert den kontinent aus der luft;
    einmal verankert, entrisse ihn
    selbst das gesamte zeppelinblau,
    das über ihn hinzieht, nicht seinem grund:

er wächst, von tau zu takelage,
    von netz zu gitter, erfaßt die form
    perfekt, umschlingt sie, schiebt sich zwischen
    all das, was wirt und nicht-wirt ist.

morgen mit dem blechzerreißenden
    kreischen eines kakaduschwarms;
    morgen mit den jalousien
    von riesenfarn und erster sonne,

die durch die lamellen dringt,
    dem teekesselpfiff eines vogels.
    von irgendwo das leise knarren
    der tür im innern eines stamms:

dort steht er, archiviert was war als leere,
    als hohlraum, aber lockt mit früchten,
    die wirklich sind und süß — der baum,
    der an die stelle eines baumes trat.

ficus watkinsiana

begins where others wish they'd end up,
    in light, rappels himself out of himself,
    hits exactly that tiny needle eye
    in the rainforest, threads itself in.

enters the continent out of the air;
    now anchored, even the whole
    zeppelin blue gliding over it
    cannot rip it from out of this ground.

it grows, from rope to rigging,
    from net to lattice, captures the form
    always perfectly; entwines it, shoves
    itself between what's host and not.

morning with the sheet metal–ripping
    screech of a cockatoo swarm;
    morning with the window shutters
    of giant fern and the first sun,

piercing through the blinds,
    the teakettle whistle of a bird.
    from somewhere comes the faintest creak
    of a door inside some trunk.

stands now grasping emptiness, a shell
    that archives what had once existed here,
    luring with a fruit that's sweet and real:
    where one tree lived, there is another.

dachshund

"Wie würden Sie, Comtesse, die Welt sehen, wenn Sie—sagen wir—
als Dachshund geboren wären?"
—JAKOB JOHANN VON UEXKÜLL ZU SEINER
ZUKÜNFTIGEN FRAU, GUDRUN VON SCHWERIN

als wald. als jagdausflug. als einen ball,
der auf mich zurollt, kurz vor meinem teppich
den haken schlägt und als hase enteilt.
als einen warmen nachmittag, der sich
    so langhin ausdehnt wie ich selbst,
      bevor erneut eine depesche

aus duft mich erreicht. es ist ein system
von zeichen: hierher!, rufen die disteln
mit ihren stachelfäustlingen, jeder stamm
enthält eine botschaft, altpapier, textilien,

sogar der aufgeplatzte fahrradschlauch
einer überfahrenen schlange.
der fuchs, der jeden abend hinterm bach
entlangschnürt, ist der sonnenuntergang.

mit der erregung des entdeckers
der fährte zu folgen, einem rehkitz,
den wölfen und ihrem beweglichen reich, dem dachs,
der schwarz und weiß gestreift wie ein lakritz-

bonbon in seinem dunkel sitzt; zu bellen,
wie eine rohrpost durch die gänge jagend,
dem scharfen dunst entgegen, ihn zu stellen:
ein plumper, ängstlicher riese, ein gigant,

dachshund

"How would you, comtessa, see the world, if you—let's say—had been born as a dachshund?"
—JAKOB JOHANN VON UEXKÜLL TO HIS
FUTURE WIFE, GUDRUN VON SCHWERIN

as a forest. a hunting trip. a ball
that rolls to me and as it reaches
my rug, takes a leap, escapes as a rabbit;
as a warm afternoon, that stretches
    and stretches farther out as i do myself,
    before another dispatch

of fragrance comes in. it is a system
of signs: hither!, shout the thistles
with their spike mittens, and every trunk portends
a message, like the wastepaper does, textiles,

even the burst bicycle tubing
of an overrun snake.
the fox that runs behind the brook
each evening is the setting sun.

with the excitement of the explorer
who follows the deer tracks,
the wolves and their movable kingdom, and the badger,
striped in black and white like licorice-stick

candy, lingering in his darkness,
to speed like a pneumatic tube through tunnels
toward the stinging smells, to hunt
him who is a giant, a plump, skittish colossus,

erstarrt in seinem mantel aus borsten,
während die stimmen sich nähern — der augenblick,
bevor sie da sind, lehm und erde bersten,
man ihn und mich nach oben reißt, ins licht.

bristling, stiffened in his coat,
while the voices come closer—at the moment
before their arrival, before they burst through clay and earth,
and the two of us are yanked into the light.

rübezahl

bäume um bäume, und dahinter ruhig
der wald, der mit den augen seiner tiere
sieht. nur ein paar bäche infiltrieren
die dämmerung, ein dünner pfeifenrauch

von nebel steigt auf. jenseits von schreiberhau
und krummhübel: im geäst
noch immer die tropfen des gewitterschau-
ers, jeder mit dem winzigen insekt

der sonne darin, als sich die schatten
der berge strecken, du endlich die vertrauten
silhouetten der getreidesilos,

das dorf erkennst: die schädelstätte
am rand des trüben ackers nur ein haufen
von zuckerrüben, ungeheuer, zahllos.

rübezahl

trees upon trees, and behind them, quietly,
dense forest, which with the eyes of his animals
sees you. only a brook intermittently
infiltrates the dusk, a thin pipe-smoke haze

of fog rising. beyond schreiberhau
and krummhübel: in the thicket,
still the drops of the thundershow-
er, each with the minuscule insect

of sunshine within it, as the shadows
of the mountains stretch out, and you finally reach
the familiar silhouettes of the grain silos,

the village: the cluster of skulls
at the dank field's edge, merely a bunch
of sugar beets, engorged, innumerable.

klatschmohn

man kann sehr lange stehen, sich gedulden,
sofern es klatschmohn gibt, seinen barocken
überschwang und jene viergeteilten
blüten zwischen weizen oder roggen,

die uns am hellen mittag plötzlich wecken,
mit allen sinnen scharf durchatmen lassen,
ein augensalmiak; kann auf den wegen
sehr lange stehen und den schatten lauschen, kann
    die landschaft wie zum ersten mal erfassen,

bis alles schatten ist und juniwärme,
nurmehr der mohn sich auf die felder legt,
in leuchtkugeln herabbrennt (in der ferne

die letzte amsel und das rattern, rattern
der güterzüge), überm abend schwebt:
hier unten sind wir, niemand muß uns retten.

field poppy

you could stand here very long, patient,
as long as there's field poppy, his baroque
exuberance and those evenly quartered
blossoms in between the wheat and the rye,

so when in midday bright we jolt awake,
with all our senses fiercely breathe him in,
a seeing-salt; you can stand here on the pathways
for a very long time and listen to the shadows, the landscape,
        as if just now having some realization,

until everything is shadow and june-ness;
and only the poppy out in the field is moving,
fizzling down like flares do (while from afar,

the last blackbird and the clatter, clatter
of the freight trains) floating on the evening:
with us down here, and no one must save us.

pieter codde: *bildnis eines mannes mit uhr*

I

kaum daß ich sie halte:
als hätte sie auf meinen fingerspitzen
sich niedergelassen, nur um kurz zu sitzen
und auszuruhen wie ein falter
von seltenem glanz,

der seine flügel öffnet, schließt,
sie öffnet, schließt,
dann golden weitertanzt.

II

ich könnte alles sein, rauhbein
und unglücksrabe, der das regennasse
gefieder schüttelt, während sein rubin
als auge in die schenke leuchtet; einer, der nur so
zum spaß zu singen anfängt, bis die pelzigen raupen
des schnurrbarts tanzen unter seiner nase;

ein tulpenspekulant, ein reeder,
der sich versteckt hält hinter butzenscheiben,
von reisen träumt nach ceylon und retour,
während die kannen in den höfen scheppern,
die kühlen milchlaternen haarlems oder rotter-
dams. vernehme ich im schlaf das schaben

der taue? muß ich weinen, wenn die graugän-
se weiterziehen, ist mein wams benetzt
von rauch und pulver dutzender von kriegen?

pieter codde: *portrait of a man with watch*

I

less do i hold this thing
than over my fingers it lies
having lowered itself, momentarily
at rest like butterfly wings
of rare brilliance,

which open, close,
and then open, close,
then, goldenly, dance.

II

i could be anything, could be the roughneck,
could be the birdbrain shaking off his rain-
wet plumage, while his ruby ring
blazes like an eye before a lantern;
one who willy-nilly starts to sing,
which makes the caterpillar mustache dance;

a tulip gambler, a head shipman,
who hides himself behind crown glass windows,
dreaming of the journeys to ceylon,
while the churns in the courtyards clatter:
cool milk-lanterns of haarlem or rotterdam.
do i hear in my sleep the scraping ropes

of ships? must i cry, when the grey geese
move on, is my doublet dusted
with the smoke and powder of dozens of wars?

ich könnte alles sein, opportunist
und ränkeschmied — der runde, weiße kragen
aus seide kunstvoll wie ein wespennest.

III

wieder geht dein blick
zurück zu dem detail: du siehst den bart
am kinn, das grau darin, und den bestick-
ten ärmelschlitz; du siehst die borte

am umgeklappten hemd, wo flocke
um flocke schnee vernäht ist, und die schläfe,
von der die locke hängt wie eine flagge
jenseits der grenze, ohne winde, schlaff.

mein breitkrempiger hut, der wie ein loch
dahinter klafft, ein tintenfäßchen
das umgekippt ist, dessen lache

sich langsam ausdehnt, deren schwarz mich einsaugt,
während das auge spricht: bleib noch ein bißchen,
perfekter falter, tickendes insekt.

i could be everything, opportunist
and intriguer—the round, white collar
of silk, as elaborate as a wasp's nest.

III

again your gaze must follow
back to the details: you see my beard
on the chin, the grey within, and the embroi-
dered sleeve with a vent; you see the border

of the folded-up shirt, where flake
after flake of snow is sewn on, and the temple,
from which a curl hangs like a flag
beyond its frontier, without wind, limp.

and my broad-brimmed hat that like a hole
yawns behind me, an inkpot,
recently knocked over, whose puddle

slowly spreads outward, whose black
absorbs me while the eye says: stay like that,
perfect butterfly, ticking insect.

koi

die ursuppe von teich, hinter den giebeln
der palmenhäuser: koi, wie sie sich drängen,
als goldene fäden einen gobelin

aus schwärze durchwirken, ihre bahnen
schwerer vorherzusagen als kometen;
das runde maul, das nichts als ihren namen

zu formen scheint, wenn sie den punkt berühren,
der luft von wasser trennt, ihr kammerton
zu hoch oder zu tief für unsere ohren,

unhörbar: koi, ein firmament aus geld
am grund des beckens, unter ihnen hängend,
verliebt ins schummrige wie jede glut,

neben dem plankenweg ein schweben, schwelen.
etwas von ihrer hünenhaften ruhe,
dem sturen herzschlag sollte übergehen

auf mich, wenn ich die hand ins dunkel halte
und warte auf den kalten stoß, das rauhe
paillettenkleid; und so beginnt das alter.

koi

in the primeval soup of lakes, behind the gables
of the palm houses: koi, as they clot,
as they weave into the tapestry of blackness

their golden threads, their orbits more
difficult to predict than comets;
the round mouth that seems to form

nothing but their name, touching the place
where air divides from water; their chamber pitch
too high or too low for our ears,

inaudible: koi, a firmament of coins
on the bottom of the pool, jangling beneath,
loving dimness like only embers can;

next to the promenade they hover, smolder;
something from their hulking calm,
from their stubborn heartbeat should transfer

upon myself, when i dip my hand into the bilge
and wait for the cold jolt, the rugged gown
of sequins, thereby beginning old age.

Notes

p. 13: *plemplem*: idiomatic phrase for "out of one's mind," "cuckoo."

p. 113: This is the Rübezahl spirit of the Sudeten Mountains, from fairy tales; a spirit you'd better not anger. "Rübezahl" literally means "Beetcount" or "Beetcounter," as that's what he does in the tale. —JW

Acknowledgments

Beltway Quarterly: "ficus watkinsiana," "dachshund," "essay on fences"

Cincinnati Review: "teabag," "amish," "quince paté," "gecko,"
"essay on gnats"

Cerise Press: "augustín lópez: the art of topiary," "december
1914," "elderflower," "oysters," "evel knievel"

Copper Nickel: "sloes," "from the globe factory," "koalas," "rain
barrel variations," "krynica morska"

Kenyon Review Online: "histories: onesilos," "in the well"

Mid-American Review: "corn," "rhino," "dobermann," "steinway,"
"pinochle," "nicosia," "wejherowo," "chameleon,"
"the merman"

Poetry International: "the west," "mushrooms," "bedsheets,"
"clover," "nail"

Poetry London: "lazarus"

Two Lines: "rübezahl" (as "beetcounter"), "koi," "pieter codde"
(parts 1-3), "field poppy"

Many of the poems in this collection were compiled from Jan
Wagner's six poetry books, including most recently *Achtzehn
Pasteten* (*Eighteen Pies*, Berlin Verlag, 2007), *Australien* (*Australia*,
Berlin Verlag, 2010), *Die Eulenhasser in den Hallenhäusern. Drei
Verborgene* (*The Owl-Haters in the Hallhouses. Three Concealed Poets*, Hanser
Berlin Verlag, 2012), and *Regentonnenvariationen* (*Rain Barrel Variations*,
Hanser Berlin Verlag, 2014).

Grateful acknowledgment to the National Endowment
for the Arts, which granted a fellowship based on the merit of
this project and which funded its completion. Thanks to Carsten
René Nielsen, who suggested this project, and to our friend
Katharina Norden, who was a strong resource in the first round
of these translations.

Alberto Novelli

JAN WAGNER is the recipient of the 2017 Georg Büchner Prize, one of Germany's most prestigious honors in literature. He has published six collections of poems since 2001, as well as two collections of essays, several edited volumes, and a number of translations. For his poetry, which has been translated into more than thirty languages, Wagner has received fellowships from the German Academy, the Villa Massimo in Rome, the Villa Aurora, and elsewhere. His literary awards include the Anna Seghers Award, the Ernst Meister Award for Poetry, and the Friedrich Hölderlin Award. A member of the German Academy of Language and Literature, Wagner lives in Berlin.

Czarina Divinagracia

DAVID KEPLINGER is the author of five volumes of poetry, most recently *Another City*. He has won the T.S. Eliot Prize, the C.P. Cavafy Poetry Prize, the Erskine J. Poetry Prize, and the Colorado Book Award, as well as two fellowships from the National Endowment for the Arts and grants from the DC, Danish, and Pennsylvania Councils on the Arts. He directs the MFA program in creative writing at American University in Washington, DC.

milkweed
editions

Founded as a nonprofit organization in 1980, Milkweed Editions is an independent publisher. Our mission is to identify, nurture and publish transformative literature, and build an engaged community around it.

milkweed.org

Interior design by Mary Austin Speaker
Typeset in Centaur (text) and Bodoni (display)

Centaur was drawn as titling capitals for a book about the mythical creature of the same name in 1914 by renowned classical typographer Bruce Rogers for the Metropolitan Museum of Art. Rogers's design for the typeface was influenced by such fifteenth-century texts as Nicholas Jenson's *Eusebius* and Pietro Bembo's *De Aetna*. The metal typeface was privately cast by the American Type Foundry and released by the Monotype Corporation in 1929.

Bauer Bodoni was designed by Heinrich Jost in 1926. During his tenure as artistic director of the Bauer Type Foundry in Frankfurt, Jost sought to replicate the typefaces originally created by Giambattista Bodoni in the eighteenth century, who was himself influenced by the designs of Francois Didot and Pierre Simon Fournier. Bodoni is known as "the king of typography and the typographer of Kings," having enjoyed the patronage of both the Duke of Parma and Napoleon Bonaparte. Bauer Bodoni is regarded as one of the most delicate and graceful Bodoni interpretations.